Oracle General Ledger R12 Interview Questions

By: Hasan Mir

handsonerp.com

Oracle General Ledger R12 Interview Questions by Hasan Mir

Oracle General Ledger R12 Interview Questions

ISBN: 978-0-557-07499-0

Copyright© 2009 Hasan Mir. All rights reserved. No part of this publication may be reproduced, stored in a retrieval system, or transmitted in any form or by any means including electronic, mechanical, photocopying, recording, or otherwise. The scanning, uploading, and distribution of this book via the internet or via any other means is illegal and punishable by law.

For video based training please visit our website at handsonerp.com.

Oracle General Ledger R12 Interview Questions by Hasan Mir

Table of Contents

About the Author..13

Introduction..14

Question 1: What is ERP? 16

Question 2: What is Oracle E-Business Suite? 16

Question 3: What is Oracle Financials? 16

Question 4: What is Oracle General Ledger? 16

Question 5: What main functionality is offered by the General Ledger module? 16

Question 6: What kind of data flows from external modules into General Ledger module? 17

Question 7: Why is it important to transfer accounting information to General Ledger module? 17

Question 8: What are the high level steps to setup General Ledger module? 18

Question 9: Explain the concept of a ledger. 18

Question 10: Explain the concept of a legal entity. 19

Question 11: What is the relationship between legal entities and ledgers in Oracle? 19

Question 12: What does a ledger consist of? 19

Question 13: What are the 4 Cs in Oracle? 20

Question 14: What are the steps involved in creating a ledger? 20

Question 15: Why do you need to define retained earnings account in the accounting setup of your ledger? 20

Oracle General Ledger R12 Interview Questions by Hasan Mir

Question 16: Explain different types of accounts. 21

Question 17: Explain debits and credits. 21

Question 18: Did we have 4 Cs in 11i as well? 22

Question 19: What does sub-ledger accounting convention mean? 22

Question 20: What is the difference between accrual accounting and cash accounting? 22

Question 21: What is a relationship between chart of account structure and segments? 23

Question 22: Explain the significance of a multiple segment chart of account structure? 23

Question 23: What is the minimum number of segments that a chart of account structure could have? 24

Question 24: What is the maximum number of segments a chart of account structure could have? 24

Question 25: Give examples of commonly implemented segments in a chart of account structure. 25

Question 26: Do you see anything wrong with these segments within a chart of account structure: Company-Account-Country-State-City? ...25

Question 27: What should be the main criteria in deciding which segments to include in the chart of account structure? 26

Question 28: What is the difference between chart of account structure and accounting flexfield? 26

Question 29: What are flexfields? 26

Question 30: How many types of flexfields are there? 26

Question 31: What is the difference between key flexfield and descriptive flexfield? 27

Question 32: What are the high level steps to create a chart of account

Oracle General Ledger R12 Interview Questions by Hasan Mir

structure? 28

Question 33: What is a value set? 29

Question 34: Why do you attach value sets to chart of account segments? 29

Question 35: Could you attach one value set to more than one segment? 29

Question 36: Can you keep books for more than one company within one ledger? 30

Question 37: What is the significance of segment qualifiers? 31

Question 38: What is the significance of a balancing segment? 31

Question 39: What are the steps involved in creating a calendar? 32

Question 40: How many years in advance do you have to create in a calendar? 32

Question 41: How far back should a calendar go in the past? 33

Question 42: What are the main rules that should be followed while creating a Calendar? 33

Question 43: What is an adjustment period? 34

Question 44: How do you define a functional currency in Oracle? 34

Question 45: What is the significance of a functional currency? 35

Question 46: Can you enter a foreign currency journal? 35

Question 47: What are different ways of providing exchange rate to Oracle while entering a foreign currency journal? 35

Question 48: What is a journal hierarchy in Oracle? 36

Question 49: Why does a journal has to have at least two lines? 36

Question 50: Is it mandatory to create batches in Oracle General Ledger? 36

Oracle General Ledger R12 Interview Questions by Hasan Mir

Question 51: Can you access more than one ledger through a single responsibility and how would you go about that? 36

Question 52: Are there any restrictions in placing ledgers in a data access set? 37

Question 53: If you wish to restrict a group of users from using particular values in a segment, then what options do you have in terms of configuration? 37

Question 54: What is a security rule? 38

Question 55: What are the steps to implement security rules? 38

Question 56: What is the difference between security rule and data access set? 38

Question 57: What is an account combination? 39

Question 58: Can a user enter any combination of values while entering journals? 39

Question 59: Why would you enable dynamic insertion? 40

Question 60: What is a cross validation rule? 40

Question 61: Lets say you create a new cross validation rule and there exists a combination in GL Accounts screen that violates this rule. Would users be able to use this combination in journal entries? 41

Question 62: What are commonly used settings with respect to dynamic insertion and cross validation rules? 41

Question 63: Lets say you have a two segment chart of account structure: COMPANY-ACCOUNT and you wish to create a cross validation rule that company 01 cannot be used with any 6 series account. What lines would you enter for this rule? 42

Question 64: What is the significance of posting a journal? 43

Question 65: Can you delete a posted journal? 43

Oracle General Ledger R12 Interview Questions by Hasan Mir

Question 66: What would you do if you have posted an incorrect journal? 43

Question 67: What is the difference between deleting a journal and reversing a journal? 43

Question 68: What is the difference between change sign reversal method and switch debit/credit reversal method? 44

Question 69: What are different ways of reversing journals? 44

Question 70: What are different ways of posting journals? 45

Question 71: What are account balances? 45

Question 72: What is the difference between PTD and YTD balances? 45

Question 73: What is the process of transferring accounting information from external sources into General Ledger module? 46

Question 74: Explain the General Ledger cycle. 47

Question 75: What are different ways of creating journals in General Ledger module? 47

Question 76: What are different period statuses in General Ledger module? 48

Question 77: Describe new features in R12 General Ledger module? 48

Question 78: What are the main differences between secondary ledgers and reporting ledgers? 52

Question 79: What is mass allocation? 52

Question 80: What are recurring journals? 53

Question 81: What are the ways of entering statistical information in Oracle like headcounts and number of units etc? 53

Question 82: What are different types of journals you can enter in a General Ledger module? 54

Oracle General Ledger R12 Interview Questions by Hasan Mir

Question 83: Can you enter a journal where debits are not equal to credits? 54

Question 84: What are budgets? 54

Question 85: What is mass budget? 55

Question 86: What is the difference between mass allocation and mass budget? 55

Question 87: What is a budget formula? 56

Question 88: What is the difference between budget formula and recurring journal formula? 56

Question 89: What are the main high level steps for setting up budgets in Oracle? 57

Question 90: What is a budget organization? 57

Question 91: Can budget organizations have overlapping GL Accounts? 58

Question 92: What are different ways of entering budgets in Oracle? 58

Question 93: What are different ways of entering budget amounts? ...59

Question 94: What are different ways of creating budget journals? 59

Question 95: What is a fund check level? 60

Question 96: What are budget groups? 60

Question 97: What does available funds mean? 61

Question 98: What are encumbrances? 61

Question 99: What are income statement accounts? 62

Question 100: What is an income statement report? 63

Question 101: What are balance sheet accounts? 63

Question 102: What is a balance sheet report? 63

Oracle General Ledger R12 Interview Questions by Hasan Mir

Question 103: What would it mean if the accounting equation is not balanced in your balance sheet? 64

Question 104: What are different types of reports that you could run in General Ledger? 64

Question 105: What are standard reports? 64

Question 106: What are FSG reports? 65

Question 107: What is a cash flow statement? 65

Question 108: Give few examples of commonly run standard reports in General Ledger. 65

Question 109: Give few examples of commonly run FSG reports that you create in Oracle. 66

Question 110: Describe mandatory components of an FSG report. 66

Question 111: Describe optional components of an FSG reports. 67

Question 112: What is an FSG report set? 67

Question 113: What are three main processes pertaining to foreign currencies in General Ledger module? 68

Question 114: Explain the process of currency conversion. 68

Question 115: Explain the process of currency translation. 69

Question 116: Explain the process of currency revaluation. 69

Question 117: What are different exchange rates that are used in conversion, translation, and revaluation? 71

Question 118: Where do you enter daily rates, period end rates, period average rates, and historical rates? 71

Question 119: What are rate types? 72

Question 120: How would you perform consolidated reporting of two companies? 72

Oracle General Ledger R12 Interview Questions by Hasan Mir

Question 121: What are the steps involved in performing a consolidation data transfer from one ledger to the other? 73

Question 122: Why is mapping required for consolidation data transfer? 73

Question 123: Explain elimination entries using an example? 74

Question 124: Explain average balancing? 74

Question 125: What does freezing a source means in Oracle General Ledger? 75

Question 126: What features are available in Account Inquiry screen for end-users? 75

Question 127: What is the significance of sequences in Oracle General Ledger module? 75

Question 128: Explain the types of sequences available in release R12. 76

Question 129: What is the significance of journal approval feature? ..76

Question 130: What are the setup steps involved in enabling journal approvals? 76

Question 131: What is a suspense account? 77

Question 132: What is an Account Hierarchy Manager? 77

Question 133: What are summary accounts? 77

Question 134: How do you create summary accounts? 78

Question 135: Lets say you are asked to create summary accounts so that one can query consolidated balances in all assets for each individual company. How would you go about that task assuming a two segment chart of account structure: COMPANY-ACCOUNT? ...78

Question 136: What formula values you can enter in a summary account template..79

Oracle General Ledger R12 Interview Questions by Hasan Mir

Question 137: What is aparent value? 79

Question 138: What is a rollup group? 80

Question 139: Can you use a parent value directly in summary account template instead of using a rollup group? 80

Question 140: Can a child value belong to more than one parent value? 80

Oracle General Ledger R12 Interview Questions by Hasan Mir

About the Author

Hasan Mir is an Oracle Financials Technical/Functional Consultant in Canada since more than 13 years. He has performed several implementations at reputed firms including Oracle Corporation, CGEY, Ontario IMO, Dofasco. He has diverse experience in providing Oracle technologies training including authoring books, providing instructor-led trainings, and conducting seminars and webinars. He runs a video-based training website handsonerp.com, offering variety of online courses on Oracle E-Business Suite.

Oracle General Ledger R12 Interview Questions by Hasan Mir

Introduction

It is extremely challenging to find precise and easy to understand guides when it comes to Oracle E-Business Suite. This makes the journey of a newcomer harder than originally perceived.

In an attempt to make things easier, and to make a contribution in providing easy to understand tutorials for Oracle Financials, I maintain a video-based training website handsonerp.com. Additionally, I wanted to write a book that not only prepares one for an interview but also serves as a easy to understand tutorial on Oracle General Ledger features. This book is a result of my efforts in this direction.

 This book will give you a tour of Oracle General Ledger module. Questions progress in a logical sequence. The answers follow a step by step, easy to understand approach. I have provided examples wherever possible. Also, I have compared release R12 with older release 11i wherever applicable in order to better equip you for comparison questions during interviews.

Who would benefit from this book?

- Potential interview candidates
- Managers
- Interviewers
- Consultants

For an experienced consultant, this book serves as a refresher of Oracle General Ledger features before an interview. For a novice, this books provides a high level tutorial on Oracle General Ledger and serves as a road map for further learning. For someone who is totally new to Oracle E-Business Suite, this book serves as an express tour of Oracle General Ledger.

I am sure you will benefit from this book and it will make a positive difference in your interviews. I look forward to get your feedback via my website: <u>handsonerp.com</u>.

Hasan Mir

Oracle General Ledger R12 Interview Questions by Hasan Mir

Question 1: What is ERP?

ERP stands for Enterprise Resource Planning. An ERP software is a complete end to end information management solution for an enterprise.

Question 2: What is Oracle E-Business Suite?

Oracle E-Business Suite, formerly known as Oracle Applications, is a leading ERP software offered by Oracle Corporation.

Question 3: What is Oracle Financials?

Oracle Financials is a group of financial modules within Oracle E-Business Suite.

Question 4: What is Oracle General Ledger?

Oracle General Ledger is one of the modules within Oracle Financials. It helps finance department of a company to manage their accounting and reporting.

Question 5: What main functionality is offered by the General Ledger module?

Oracle General Ledger module is a financial management solution within Oracle E-Business Suite and a central repository for accounting information. The General Ledger module mainly helps you manage journals, budgets, and financial reports. It is used by the finance department of an enterprise.

Question 6: What kind of data flows from external modules into General Ledger module?

Most modules in Oracle E-Business Suite record business transactions and as a result generate accounting information. The accounting information is then transferred to General Ledger module at period end.

For example, when you enter an invoice in Payables module, an accounting entry is generated reflecting the increase in expense and an increase in liability. When you pay this invoice, another entry is generated reflecting a decrease in cash and decrease in liability. All the accounting entries must be sent over to General Ledger module so that they are reflected in the financial reports.

Question 7: Why is it important to transfer accounting information to General Ledger module?

Financial reports are run out of General Ledger module. The reports display accounting information. Financial reports are of paramount importance to the stakeholders as the numbers reflect the health and performance of the company.

If all accounting information is not sent over to General Ledger module, the reports would not reflect the true picture.

Oracle General Ledger R12 Interview Questions by Hasan Mir

Question 8: What are the high level steps to setup General Ledger module?

These are the high level steps to setup General Ledger module:

- Create ledgers
- Create responsibilities
- Set profile options
- Assign responsibilities to users
- Open the first period
- Configure rest of the features based on client's requirements including consolidations, suspense accounts, summary accounts, allocations, budgets, secondary ledgers, reporting currencies, approvals etc.

Question 9: Explain the concept of a ledger.

A ledger is an accounting representation for one or more legal entities or for a business need.

You can imagine a ledger as a book in which you enter journals. The data in a General Ledger module is segregated by ledgers; hence you only see journals that were entered in the ledger you have signed into.

In 11i, ledgers were referred as "set of books".

Oracle General Ledger R12 Interview Questions by Hasan Mir

Question 10: Explain the concept of a legal entity.

A legal entity is a business unit where fiscal and tax reports are prepared. It is an entity that is registered with the tax authorities and it is given a unique tax identifier.

In Oracle, a legal entity owns centralized tax setup, bank accounts, and sub-ledger transactions.

Question 11: What is the relationship between legal entities and ledgers in Oracle?

There is a one-to-many relationship between legal entities and ledgers.

The whole ledger could be declared as one legal entity or individual balancing segment values within a ledger could be declared as one legal entity. In the latter case a ledger would consist of multiple legal entities.

In either case you are able to produce financial statements, like income statements and balance sheets, at the legal entity level.

Question 12: What does a ledger consist of?

Main attributes of a ledger include:

- Chart of Account Structure
- Calendar
- Functional Currency

- Sub-ledger Accounting Convention

Question 13: What are the 4 Cs in Oracle?

The main components of a ledger are sometimes referred to as 4 Cs.

- (C)hart of Account Structure
- (C)alendar
- Functional (C)urrency
- Sub-ledger Accounting (C)onvention

Question 14: What are the steps involved in creating a ledger?

At a minimum, you must create a chart of account structure, calendar, and you must enable your functional currency.

While defining the accounting setup for your ledger you would be asked to specify your retained earnings account. Therefore values must exist in value sets attached to the segments in your chart of account structure.

Question 15: Why do you need to define retained earnings account in the accounting setup of your ledger?

Balances in expense and revenue accounts are closed in the retained earnings accounts by Oracle, as of end of the year. That is why one must specify retained earnings account at the ledger level.

Question 16: Explain different types of accounts.

GL Accounts could be of the following types:

- Asset: Things of value that the company owns.
- Liability: Obligations of your company to other business units.
- Equity: Interest of owners in the business.
- Revenue: Cash inflow as a result of selling goods or services.
- Expense: Cost incurred in the process of running the business.

Question 17: Explain debits and credits.

Every accounting entry in General Ledger contains both debit as well as credit amounts. All debits must equal all credits within an journal.

Depending on what type of account you are dealing with, a debit or credit will either increase or decrease the account balance.

- A debit will increase the balance in assets and expense accounts, while a credit will do the opposite.
- Similarly a credit will increase the balance in liabilities, equity, and revenue accounts while a debit will perform the opposite function.

Oracle General Ledger R12 Interview Questions by Hasan Mir

Question 18: Did we have 4 Cs in 11i as well?

In Oracle R12 we have 4 Cs. In Oracle 11i we had 3 Cs. The sub-ledger accounting convention functionality was there but it was configured at the sub-ledger level, not at the General Ledger level. In Oracle R12 the accounting convention is specified at the ledger level.

Question 19: What does sub-ledger accounting convention mean?

Two types of Accounting entries could be produced at sub-ledger level:

- Accrual Accounting
- Cash Accounting

The sub-ledger accounting convention choice dictates which type of accounting entries would be generated.

Question 20: What is the difference between accrual accounting and cash accounting?

In accrual accounting convention, expenses and revenues are recognized in the period in which the business event took place irrespective of the actual cash inflow and the outflow. In cash accounting convention, expenses and revenues are recognized in the period when the actual cash outflow or inflow has taken place irrespective of when the business event occurred.

For example, if a company purchased $100 worth of office supplies in January and made a payment in

February then according to the accrual accounting the expense has incurred in January but according to cash accounting convention the expense has incurred in February.

Question 21: What is a relationship between chart of account structure and segments?

A chart of account structure consists of segments. It is also referred to as a multiple segment chart of account structure since it contains multiple segments. A segment represents a business dimension that you wish to capture during data entry.

Question 22: Explain the significance of a multiple segment chart of account structure?

In a traditional accounting system you would only capture debit or credit activity against natural account numbers e.g. 1000, 2000 etc.

In Oracle, besides account numbers you can also capture other dimensions that are crucial for the client from a reporting perspective. This way users could perform balance inquiries based on any dimension.

For example a user can inquire on net cash activity that took place during the previous month for a renovation project in the marketing department. While in a traditional system, the same user could only inquire on total cash activity that took place in the previous month. The breakdown by department and project would not be possible.

Oracle General Ledger R12 Interview Questions by Hasan Mir

Before you start using Oracle General Ledger module, you need to define all the dimensions that you would like to capture during data entry. You define segments to represent dimensions e.g. project, department, product etc. The chart of account structure is a group of these segments.

Question 23: What is the minimum number of segments that a chart of account structure could have?

A chart of account structure must contain the following segments:

- Balancing Segment
- Natural Account

Therefore the minimum number of segments that a chart of account structure could have is two.

Question 24: What is the maximum number of segments a chart of account structure could have?

Oracle allows a maximum of 30 segments in a chart of account structure. However, it is not advisable to have more than 7 segments, since a large number of segments may slow down the data entry.

Oracle General Ledger R12 Interview Questions by Hasan Mir

Question 25: Give examples of commonly implemented segments in a chart of account structure.

Here are few examples:

- Company
- Account
- Department
- Project
- LOB (Line of Business)
- Product
- Cost Center
- Region

Question 26: Do you see anything wrong with these segments within a chart of account structure: Company-Account-Country-State-City?

Yes, this structure is not correct. If a value of one segment could be derived from a value of the other segment then that segment should not be part of the structure. Here state could be derived from the city and country could be derived from the state and also could be derived from the city. The segments country and state are redundant.

Question 27: What should be the main criteria in deciding which segments to include in the chart of account structure?

The reporting requirement of the client is the most important criteria for deciding the segments of the structure. You need to evaluate what dimensions of the business the client wishes to see in the reports.

Question 28: What is the difference between chart of account structure and accounting flexfield?

Accounting flexfield is also called chart of account structure. The two terms are synonyms.

Accounting flexfield is more of a technical term while the term chart of account structure is commonly used in business context.

Question 29: What are flexfields?

Flexfield is a technology that lets users enter more than one value in a single field. The number of values that would be entered in a single field could vary from client to client based on their requirements.

Question 30: How many types of flexfields are there?

There are two types of flexfields:

- Key Flexfield
- Descriptive Flexfield

Question 31: What is the difference between key flexfield and descriptive flexfield?

Key flexfields allow you to enter multiple segment values that have special meaning to Oracle and that are tied to the core functionality of the application. For example, account numbers in General Ledger module, asset keys and asset categories in Assets module etc.

Following is an example of an account number:

- 01-1000-01 (COMPANY-ACCOUNT-DEPARTMENT)

An account number may consist of multiple values. The number of segments would differ from one client to the other.

Account numbers are tied to the core functionality of the application. For instance, account numbers are displayed in General Ledger reports, users could perform inquiries on account numbers through the Account Inquiry screen, and posting program posts balances in account numbers etc.

On the other hand, the sole purpose of descriptive flexfields is to enable extra fields on a screen without any programming. This way users can enter extra information in these fields. Oracle would store the extra information in the database but this information is not tied to any core functionality of the application, as in the case of key flexfields.

For instance, you can enable descriptive flexfield on Customer screen in Receivables module, in order to let users store customers color and sizing preferences. As a result extra fields would be enabled on that screen. Following is an example of information that you could enter in the extra fields:

- Red-Large (COLOR-SIZE)

Oracle would simply store these values in the database. These values are not tied to any functionality of the application.

The purpose of both types of flexfields is the same, that is to enable users to enter multiple values in a single field.

Question 32: What are the high level steps to create a chart of account structure?

These are the high level steps to create a chart of account structure:

- Create value sets.
- Define the structure.
- Define segments within the structure and attach value sets to the segments.
- Define segment qualifiers.
- Enter values in the value sets.

Oracle General Ledger R12 Interview Questions by Hasan Mir

Question 33: What is a value set?

A value set is a set of values. In other words a value set is a placeholder that contains values.

Question 34: Why do you attach value sets to chart of account segments?

The main idea behind attaching a value set to the segment is that users should be restricted to use predefined values in that segment rather than entering free-style account numbers. A value set is the list of predefined legal values.

For example consider this account number: 01-1000 (COMPANY-ACCOUNT)

Lets say the value set associated with the company segment contains values 01,02,03. Users could choose only one of these values during data entry. Value 01 was selected by the user in this case for the company segment.

Question 35: Could you attach one value set to more than one segment?

Yes one value set could be attached to more than one segment of the same chart of account structure or to multiple chart of account structures. Company segment and inter-company segment are good examples. Usually the same value set is attached to the two segments. The company segment keeps track of which company is doing the transaction and inter-company segment keeps track of which company is on the other side of the transaction. The inter-company segment is usually used in enterprises where subsidiary companies do business among each other.

Question 36: Can you keep books for more than one company within one ledger?

Yes you can keep books for more than one company within one ledger. This is only possible if all companies share the same 4 Cs. Even if 1 C is different for a company then that it could not be put in the same ledger as other companies.

Lets say you have 4 companies. Functional currency of one of them is USD while for the rest of the three is CAD. All companies use the same calendar, chart of account structure including segments values, and accounting conventions. You need two ledgers because functional currency of one company is different than the rest of the three.

Lets consider another example. You have 4 companies. All of them use USD as their functional currency. All companies uses the same chart of account structure including segments values and same accounting conventions. However one of the companies uses a weekly calendar as opposed to a monthly calendar. You would need two ledgers again.

Question 37: What is the significance of segment qualifiers?

Segment qualifiers window lets you qualify your segments as balancing segment, natural account segment, management segment, cost center segment, and inter-company segment. It is mandatory that you mark one segment as balancing segment and one segment as natural account segment. The rest of the qualifiers are optional.

Question 38: What is the significance of a balancing segment?

The accounting equation ASSETS - LIABILITIES = EQUITY must remain true not only for the whole ledger but also for each value in the balancing segment.

Values within a balancing segment represent individual companies.

You can run financial statements for an individual company within the ledger as well as for the whole ledger. That is why it is important that the accounting equation remains balanced for each company.

Usually "company" segment is marked as a balancing segment. Once you qualify one of the segments as a balancing segment, Oracle ensures that no such journal is entered that throws this equation off for any individual balancing segment value.

As long as debits remain equal to credits at journal level, the accounting equation automatically remains balanced.

Oracle enforces validation that debits remain equal to credits at the journal level as well as for each balancing segment value within a journal.

Question 39: What are the steps involved in creating a calendar?

These are the steps to create a calendar:

- First you make sure that the required period type exists in Oracle. Commonly used period types are already defined as seeded data. If the required type does not exist then you need to create one.
- Then you create the accounting calendar by defining all the periods within each year one by one.

Question 40: How many years in advance do you have to create in a calendar?

Only the current year must be created in full in a calendar. You may add the next year any time before you need to open the first period of the next year.

If you are planning to maintain budgets in advance for future years, then future years must be created in advance in the calendar.

Question 41: How far back should a calendar go in the past?

If you are planning to migrate legacy data into a new implementation then you must start your calendar from a year that corresponds to the oldest period in the legacy data set.

Once you open your first General Ledger period, you cannot go back further. Therefore it is important that you choose your first period diligently.

It is always a good idea to take your calendar one year further back then the required start date. For example if JAN-09 is the first period in your legacy data set then start your calendar from JAN-08 and open JAN-08 as the first period in GL.

Question 42: What are the main rules that should be followed while creating a Calendar?

Following rules should be followed:

- Periods cannot overlap, except for adjustment periods.
- There cannot be gaps with a year.

Once you create a calendar, Oracle runs a validation on your calendar. The validation report informs you of violations if any.

Question 43: What is an adjustment period?

Accountants enter year-end adjustment entries in an adjustment period. Adjustment entries are made to update or correct the balances and to bring the numbers closer to reality.

An adjustment period is usually defined as a 13th period in a 12 month year. Its duration is one day rather than a month. Its start and end date is usually kept as 31st December.

You mark this period as "adjustment" so that Oracle lets you overlap this period with other non-adjustment periods. Only adjustment periods could overlap other periods.

Not all companies enter adjustment entries in a special 13th period. Adjustment entries could be entered in regular periods as well.

Question 44: How do you define a functional currency in Oracle?

You simply go to the currency screen and enable your functional currency. Besides enabling functional currency, you also enable all those currencies that your company would be dealing with in day-to-day business affairs. All other currencies should be disabled.

While creating a ledger you have to specify your functional currency. You choose your functional currency from the list of all enabled currencies.

Question 45: What is the significance of a functional currency?

Functional currency is a default currency for journals. Balances are stored in the database in a functional currency.

Question 46: Can you enter a foreign currency journal?

Yes, you can enter a foreign currency journal. However you would need to provide an exchange rate. Oracle converts the foreign currency amounts into functional currency amounts based on the exchange rate provided.

Question 47: What are different ways of providing exchange rate to Oracle while entering a foreign currency journal?

One way of providing an exchange rate is to enter it at the time of journal entry. This rate is called a "User Rate".

If you enter frequent foreign currency journals then you could store exchange rates in advance. Multiple versions of exchange rate databases could be created. For example group 1 could store their own exchange rates while group 2 could store their own. These versions of exchange rates are called "Rate Types".

While entering a foreign currency journal, all you need to do is pick your rate type and Oracle will retrieve the exchange rate automatically that is stored within this "version" for that date.

Question 48: What is a journal hierarchy in Oracle?

Journal batches are at the highest level in the hierarchy. A batch could have one or more headers or journals within it. A journal could have two or more lines within it.

Question 49: Why does a journal has to have at least two lines?

All debits must equal to all credits within a journal. This is a basic accounting principle. This is only possible if we have at least one debit and one credit line.

Oracle will not let you post any journal that violates this rule.

Question 50: Is it mandatory to create batches in Oracle General Ledger?

You can create a journal directly without creating a batch. However Oracle will create a batch on your behalf and will assign it a name using its default format.

Question 51: Can you access more than one ledger through a single responsibility and how would you go about that?

Yes you can do access more than one ledger using a

single responsibility in release R12. This was not possible in 11i. You assign the desired ledgers to a data access set. You assign the data access set to a responsibility. All the ledgers within the data access set would now be visible to a person signed in through this responsibility.

Question 52: Are there any restrictions in placing ledgers in a data access set?

All ledgers belonging to a single data access set must have the same calendar and chart of account structure associated with them. However, they could differ in functional currencies.

Question 53: If you wish to restrict a group of users from using particular values in a segment, then what options do you have in terms of configuration?

This could be done in two ways:

- Create security rules on that segment restricting users on particular values. Assign the rules to the responsibility.
- Create a data access set restricting access on particular balancing segment values or management segment values. Assign the set to the responsibility.

Question 54: What is a security rule?

Security Rule is a feature of Oracle that could be used to restrict a group of users from accessing any set of values in any segment.

Question 55: What are the steps to implement security rules?

First you enable security at the value set level and also at the segment level.

Then you create security rules, and assign them to the responsibility.

Users accessing the system using this responsibility would see these rules enforced.

Question 56: What is the difference between security rule and data access set?

- Security rules could be used to restrict any set of values in any segment from a group of users.
- Data access set restricts access by ledgers and also by balancing segment values or management segment values.

The only common factor between the two is that both may be used to restrict access on values in balancing segment or management segment.

Security rule could be used to restrict access on values on other segments as well besides balancing segment and management segment; whereas data access set cannot perform this function.

Security rule cannot be used to restrict access by ledgers, whereas data access set is able to do this.

Data access set is a new feature in R12.

Question 57: What is an account combination?

A combination of values in all segments of a chart of account structure is called an account combination. Oracle refers to the whole account combination as an account.

While entering a journal line, you pick up one value for each segment in your structure. The combination of values that you have picked for all segments is called an account combination. For example, 01-10000-01 and 01-20000-02 (COMPANY-ACCOUNT-DEPARTMENT).

Question 58: Can a user enter any combination of values while entering journals?

Only those combinations may be entered in a journal that are predefined in the GL Accounts screen.

If dynamic insertion is enabled, then Oracle will allow you to enter any combination you like. If the combination does not already exist in the GL Accounts screen, then it would automatically be inserted there without having someone manually add it.

Question 59: Why would you enable dynamic insertion?

Dynamic insertion is enabled if the client decides not to predefine all valid combinations in the GL Accounts screen beforehand. This way Oracle lets users enter any combination they wish, provided no cross validation rules are violated.

Question 60: What is a cross validation rule?

Cross validation rule is a feature of Oracle that allows you to define all illegal combinations in terms of "include" and "exclude" ranges.

For example, the following business rules could easily be implemented using cross validation rules:

- Company 01 cannot use any 6 series account.
- Company 02 cannot take part in projects 05 and 06.
- Company 03 does not have departments 02 and 03.
- Companies 02 and 03 cannot take part in project 07.

A combination cannot be inserted in GL Accounts screen if it violates any cross validation rule, irrespective of dynamic insertions' setting.

Oracle General Ledger R12 Interview Questions by Hasan Mir

Question 61: Lets say you create a new cross validation rule and there exists a combination in GL Accounts screen that violates this rule. Would users be able to use this combination in journal entries?

Yes, users may use any enabled combination that exists in GL Accounts screen even if it violates the newly created cross validation rule.

After creating a cross validation rule, no new combination could be entered in GL Accounts screen that violates this rule. However, existing combinations remain enabled in the system even if they violate the new rule.

That is why whenever you create a cross validation rule, you must manually disable all existing combinations in the GL Accounts screen that violates this new rule.

Question 62: What are commonly used settings with respect to dynamic insertion and cross validation rules?

The objective of all strategies is to prevent users from entering illegal combinations. Here are some commonly used strategies:

- One strategy is to enable dynamic insertion and to create cross validation rules. The net result is that Oracle lets you enter any combination as long as it is not violating the cross validation rules. This strategy is good for clients who wish to enforce business rules solely by cross validation rules and

who could define illegal combinations in terms of "include" and "exclude" ranges.
- Another common strategy is to enable dynamic insertion for few months, say 3 months, and then disable it later. No cross validation rules are defined. The net result is that after 3 months users could only use those combinations in journals that were used in the first three months. The assumption is that if a combination is not used within first 3 months then most likely it is not a valid combination. If they still wish to use a new combination then it must be manually entered in the GL Accounts screen first. This strategy is good for clients who wish to enforce business rules solely by predefining all valid combinations in GL Accounts screen and who use more or less the same combinations in journal entries from period to period.

Question 63: Lets say you have a two segment chart of account structure: COMPANY-ACCOUNT and you wish to create a cross validation rule that company 01 cannot be used with any 6 series account. What lines would you enter for this rule?

- In line 1, everything would be included first: INCLUDE From 00-0000 To ZZ-ZZZZ
- In line 2, illegal combinations would be excluded: EXCLUDE From 01-3000 To 01-3999

Oracle recommends that you include everything first, then you exclude illegal ranges.

Question 64: What is the significance of posting a journal?

When you post a journal, balances are updated. Also you cannot deleted a posted journal.

Question 65: Can you delete a posted journal?

A posted journal cannot be deleted. Only journals that have not been posted may be deleted.

Question 66: What would you do if you have posted an incorrect journal?

Since a posted journal cannot be deleted, the only option you have is to reverse the journal and post the reversal.

Question 67: What is the difference between deleting a journal and reversing a journal?

Deleting a journal removes all traces of the journal from journal tables.

However, reversing a journal keeps the original journal in the system and in addition a new journal is created which is the exact opposite of the original journal in terms of debit and credit amounts. As a result once you post the reversal journal, it nullifies the effect of the original journal on balances.

Question 68: What is the difference between change sign reversal method and switch debit/credit reversal method?

Change sign method creates a reversal journal such that the signs of line amounts are switched as compared to the original journal. For example, $10 debit becomes -$10 debit and $10 credit becomes -$10 credit.

Switch debit/credit method creates a reversal journal such that the debit and credit amounts are switched as compared to the original journal. For example, $10 debit becomes $10 credit and $10 credit becomes $10 debit.

Both methods produce the same result. The effect of the original journal is nullified from balances.

Question 69: What are different ways of reversing journals?

Here are few ways of reversing journals:

- You can reverse individual batches or journals from Enter Journals screen by clicking on Reverse button.
- If you need to reverse multiple journals then you can do that from Reversal Journals screen which allows multiple journal selection.
- If you wish to reverse all journals in a period belonging to specific categories then you can use auto reverse set feature. Either you can manually run an auto reverse set or you can attach the set to the ledger; this way it run automatically when

you close the period.

Question 70: What are different ways of posting journals?

Here are few ways of posting journals:

- You can post individual batches or journals from Enter Journals screen by clicking on Post button.
- If you need to post multiple journals then you can do that from Post screen which allows multiple journal selection.
- If you wish to post all journals in a period belonging to specific sources and categories then you can use auto post set feature. When you run an auto post set, all journals that meets the criteria are automatically posted.

Question 71: What are account balances?

You enter debit and credit amounts against accounts during journal entry. Net activity in an account is referred to as an account balance. Net activity is the sum of all debits minus the sum of all credits.

Question 72: What is the difference between PTD and YTD balances?

PTD or period-to-date balance means net activity in an account within a given period. Period is usually set equal to a month.

YTD or year-to-date balance means net activity in an account from the beginning of time till the end of the given period.

For example, lets say you started a business in JAN-09. You debited the cash account by $10 and $20 in JAN-09 by $10 in FEB-09.

PTD balance for cash account for JAN-09 is $30 and for FEB-09 is $10.

YTD balance for cash account for JAN-09 is $30 and for FEB-09 is $40.

Since all income statement accounts are closed into retained earnings account at the end of each year, YTD balance for an income statement account means net activity from the beginning of that year to the end of that period. While YTD balance for a balance sheet account means net activity from the beginning of time to the end of that period.

Question 73: What is the process of transferring accounting information from external sources into General Ledger module?

The high level process looks like this:

- The accounting data is first inserted into GL Interface table.
- The only program that is allowed to transfer data from GL Interface table into core General Ledger tables is the Journal Import program. This program validates if data is correct before bringing the data into GL.
- The import program could be launched by either

the external module or from within the General Ledger module.

Question 74: Explain the General Ledger cycle.

These are the high level steps in a General Ledger cycle:

- Next period is opened.
- Journals are entered, imported, or generated into that period.
- Journals are reviewed.
- Journals are posted.
- Consolidation is run if required.
- Revaluation and translation is run if required.
- Balances are reviewed.
- Correction journals are entered and posted if need be.
- The period is closed.
- Financial reports are issued to the stakeholders.

Question 75: What are different ways of creating journals in General Ledger module?

Different ways of creating journals in General Ledger module include:

- Journals could be entered using Enter Journal screen.
- Journals could be generated using mass allocations and recurring formulas.
- Reversal journals could be generated either manually or automatically using Auto Reverse Set.
- Journals could be imported from external modules

through GL Interface table.
- Journals could be entered in Excel sheet using Journal Wizard.

Question 76: What are different period statuses in General Ledger module?

A period could have one of the following statuses:

- Future Enterable: Journals could be entered but could not be posted.
- Open: Journals could be entered and could also be posted.
- Close: Journals could not be entered and could not be posted unless you open the period.
- Permanently Close - Same as "Close" except that you cannot re-open this period again.

Question 77: Describe new features in R12 General Ledger module?

Here are some of the new features:

- Set of books are now called ledgers. A central workbench called Accounting Setup Manager is now available in R12 that lets you perform common financial components setup from one central location. Using Accounting Setup Manager, you can setup and maintain components like: legal entities, primary ledgers, secondary ledgers, operating units, reporting currencies, sub-ledger accounting options, inter-company accounts, accounting and reporting sequences.

Oracle General Ledger R12 Interview Questions by Hasan Mir

- R12 allows you to map a legal entity to an entire ledger or to balancing segment values within a ledger. This provides a more realistic model.
- Set of books in 11i was defined by following 3 Cs:
  - Chart of Accounts
  - Functional Currency
  - Accounting Calendar

  In R12, the ledger is defined by an additional 4th C: the sub-ledger accounting convention. In 11i the sub-ledger accounting convention was defined at the operating unit level, but in R12 it is defined at the ledger level.
- Now you can access more than one ledger using a single responsibility given that all those ledgers share the same calendar and chart of account structure. First you assign ledgers to a data access set, which is a new concept introduced in R12, and then you assign the data access set to a responsibility. This way users don't have to switch responsibilities in order to access other ledgers.
- Journal lines reconciliation utility has been created in R12 that enables you to reconcile lines that should net to zero with respect to clearing accounts like suspense account, payroll payable, tax payable etc. Using the reconciliation screen, you can mark all those journal lines that bring the account balance back to zero. You can save this selection for future reference. This way you know which journal lines netted the account balance to zero.
- The features of multiple reporting currency (MRC) and journal translations have been placed under a broader concept called reporting currency. Using reporting currency feature you can create reporting ledgers at three different levels:

summary level which is comparable to release 11i journal translation, journal level which is comparable to release 11i MRC, and also at sub-ledger level which is a new option in R12.
- A new feature called secondary ledger is introduced in R12 that lets you maintain different representations of your primary ledger that could differ with the primary ledger in functional currency, calendar, and/or chart of account structure.
- A new security feature called "access set" has been introduced in R12 that lets you secure your setup components and definitions by granting specific privileges to users to view, modify, and/or execute a definition. Definitions that have this security available include: allocation and recurring formulas, calendars, auto post and auto reversal sets, budget organizations, account mappings, consolidation definitions and sets, rate types and revaluation sets.
- A new segment qualifier called management segment is available in R12. You can control data entry and reporting security by management segment or balancing segment using data access set.
- There is no need to install Application Desktop Integrator (ADI) as a desktop client software any more. Journal Wizard and Budget Wizard replacement features are now available as part of a web-based application.
- Financial Statement Generator reports could now be run across ledgers.
- In order to cater the need for legal compliance in some countries, R12 offers two mutually exclusive journal sequencing options: accounting and

reporting sequence.
- R12 lets you create recurring journals using foreign currencies.
- R12 lets you perform certain tasks across ledgers including opening and closing a period, running translation programs, and running FSG reports.
- R12 lets you allocate financial data across ledger using allocation formulas.
- You can now share auto post and auto reverse criteria sets across multiple ledgers.
- Now you can now copy entire journal batches.
- In R12 you define consolidation mapping between two chart of accounts rather than two sets of books which is a more realistic approach and could save you from defining redundant mappings.
- In R12 you can define a replacement account for a disabled account. The Journal import program replaces the disabled account with the replacement account and continues the import process. This prevent import errors.
- R12 does not allow you to reverse journals from frozen sources. This keeps the sub-ledgers synchronized with General Ledger.
- R12 does not allow you to reverse unposted journal. This ensures data integrity. In 11i it was possible to reverse a journal and delete the original journal.
- In R12, Oracle General Ledger's Account Analysis, General Journals and Trial Balance standard reports are integrated with XML Publisher.

Question 78: What are the main differences between secondary ledgers and reporting ledgers?

Following are main differences between secondary ledgers and reporting ledgers:

- Secondary ledgers could differ in any of the 4 Cs with the primary ledger. Reporting ledgers could differ only in functional currency.
- When journals are posted in primary ledger, they are automatically transferred and posted in the reporting ledgers, however they are only transferred to the secondary ledgers, but not posted. You have to manually post them in secondary ledgers.
- When you create a reporting currency ledger then it is automatically added in the default data access set associated with your primary ledger. That way you have an immediate access to the reporting ledger through your default General Ledger responsibility. In case of secondary ledgers you need to configure data access sets before you access them.

Question 79: What is mass allocation?

Mass Allocations is a feature of Oracle where you can define a formula for transferring cost from a large pool into individual accounts based on some factors.

For example, lets say your head office has made a big expenditure. The cost needs to be divided among the departments based on some factor like number of employees within each department. You can use the mass allocation formula to generate a journal that would divide the cost among the departments based on headcounts given that you have a department segment in your chart of account structure and you are keeping track of headcounts in Oracle using STAT currency.

Question 80: What are recurring journals?

In cases where certain transactions are repeated every accounting period, you can define a recurring journal formula to generate similar journals automatically each period. You can create two types of formulas, skeleton and standard. In skeleton formula amounts are not defined. Users will have to enter amounts directly in the journals once they are generated. Standard formula contains amounts as well. In a formula, you can refer to PTD or YTD balances, actual, budget or encumbrance amounts, in any account for any period. Thus you can write a simple formula with fixed amounts or you can write a complex formula where amounts are derived from existing balances.

Question 81: What are the ways of entering statistical information in Oracle like headcounts and number of units etc?

There are two ways of entering statistical information:

- You can define unit of measures for selected accounts. Once that is done, you can enter statistical information as well in your journals along with financial amounts, only for those accounts for which unit of measures are defined.

- The other way is to enable STAT currency and simply enter a journal in STAT currency. In an STAT currency journal you can only enter statistical information. Financial amounts cannot be entered.

Question 82: What are different types of journals you can enter in a General Ledger module?

You can enter following types of journals:

- Actual Journals
- STAT Journals
- Budget Journals
- Encumbrance Journals

Question 83: Can you enter a journal where debits are not equal to credits?

Debits must be equal to credits for actual journals. Otherwise you will not be able to post the journals.

This rule does not apply of other journal types like STAT, Budget, and Encumbrance. For these types you can enter a single line journal as well.

Question 84: What are budgets?

Budgets are estimates of future balances.

For example, based on previous trends you may estimate that you would be spending $100 in monthly office supplies for next 12 months. You may also estimate that you will make $1000 in consulting revenue each month for the next 12 months.

You can enter the estimates as budget amounts in Oracle. That way you can compare your actual activity with your estimated amounts.

Oracle lets you enter one or more budgets. This way each manager can store their own estimates in the system and each manager can run the reports against their own estimates. One budget version has to be designated as "current". That means this budget would appear as a default selection in most of the reports.

Oracle lets you compare the actual activity with any budget, in reports as well as using the Account Inquiry screen.

Question 85: What is mass budget?

Mass budget is a similar concept as mass allocation. Mass budget formula is used to reallocate budget amount from one large pool into individual accounts using some factor.

Question 86: What is the difference between mass allocation and mass budget?

Mass allocation formula is used to reallocate actual amounts from one large pool into individual accounts using some factor. Once you run a mass allocation formula an actual journal is generated. You can review and post the journal.

Mass budget formula is used to reallocate budget amounts from one large pool into individual accounts using some factor. Once you run a mass budget formula a budget journal is generated. You can review and post the journal.

Question 87: What is a budget formula?

You can use budget formula to general budget amounts based on a formula. In a formula, you can refer to PTD or YTD balances, actual, budget or encumbrance amounts, in any account, and for any period. Thus you can write a simple formula with fixed amounts or you can write a complex formula where amounts are derived from existing balances.

When you run a budget formula, budget amounts are directly updated. Budget journal is not generated as in case of recurring journal formulas.

Question 88: What is the difference between budget formula and recurring journal formula?

While the concept is the same and the way formulas are entered is the same as well, but there is one main difference between the two.

- When a budget formula is executed, budget amounts are updated directly in the system. Budget journals are not generated. When a recurring journal formula is executed, actual journals are produced. You can review the generated journals and post them.

Question 89: What are the main high level steps for setting up budgets in Oracle?

High level steps for setting up budgets in Oracle are:

- Define one or more budgets to represent different versions of estimated amounts that you wish to enter for a range of periods.
- Create one or more budget organizations to represent groups of accounts against which you wish to enter budget data.
- Assign General Ledger accounts to the budget organization.
- Run Maintain Budget Organization program so that account assignment could take affect.
- Open first year for the budget.
- Enter budget amounts against a particular budget and organization.
- Freeze budget.
- Run reports.

Question 90: What is a budget organization?

A budget organization is a group of GL accounts against which you would like to manage the budget amounts. You can password protect organizations. This way different managers could be given control over different organizations.

You enter budget amounts against a particular budget and a particular organization. Only those accounts are available for budget entry that are part of the organization that you have chosen.

You can create multiple organizations to represent cost centers, departments, projects, or any other business groups.

Question 91: Can budget organizations have overlapping GL Accounts?

Not all accounts have to belong to any organization, however accounts cannot overlap among organizations. The only exception is a special "ALL" organization that by default contains all GL accounts. If your company does not have a need for creating multiple budget organizations then you can use the default ALL organization.

Question 92: What are different ways of entering budgets in Oracle?

Budgets could be entered broadly in two ways:

- You can enter budget amounts directly into Budget Amounts screen. This option does not give you an audit trail. All you see is the final amounts. You cannot view the history of changes.
- You can enter and post budget journals. This option gives you an audit trail. You can see the trail of changes by looking at the journals.

You can choose to enforce budget journals options so that system does not allow anyone to enter budget amounts directly. This way you would have an audit trail available.

If you choose to enable budgetary control for your ledger then you are forced to use the budget journal method for entering budgets.

Question 93: What are different ways of entering budget amounts?

Budget amounts could be entered in following ways:

- By entering amounts directly in the system using Budget Amounts screen.
- By entering amounts in Budget Wizard which provides an Excel interface.
- By generate budget amounts through budget formulas.
- By importing amounts from an external source through Budget Interface.

Question 94: What are different ways of creating budget journals?

Budget journals could be entered in following ways:

- By entering budget journals manually in the system using Enter Budget journals screen.
- By entering budget journals in Journal Wizard which provides an Excel interface.
- By importing budget journals from an external source through GL Interface.
- By generating budget journals through Mass

Budget formula.

Question 95: What is a fund check level?

Funds check level controls the severity of budgetary control checks. It dictates what to do if sufficient funds are not available.

Three levels are available for fund checking:

- None: No fund checking takes place.
- Advisory: When transactions fail funds checking, you are notified online. You would still be able to reserve funds.
- Absolute: You will be prohibited from reserving funds for a transaction unless funds are available.

You can assign fund check level to range of accounts, to journal source and category combination, and to summary account templates.

Question 96: What are budget groups?

You can specify different fund check level for each unique combination of journal sources and categories, along with tolerances.

You group all these entries in a budget group. Multiple budget groups could be created if need be.

Budget group is simply a listing of sources and categories along with the fund check level and tolerance.

You assign budget groups to users through profile options. This way you can implement different fund check levels for different group of users.

For example you can create budget group 1 with these entries:

- Source: Payables, Fund Check Level: Advisory
- Source: Receivables, Fund Check Level: Advisory

You can create group 2 with these entries:

- Source: Payables, Fund Check Level: None
- Source: Receivables, Fund Check Level: Advisory

Now you can assign group 1 to user 1 and group 2 to user 2. This way user 1 would face different fund check level than user 2 for Payables.

Question 97: What does available funds mean?

Available Funds = Actual - Budgets - Encumbrances

Question 98: What are encumbrances?

Encumbrances are commitments that have not been converted into actual expenses yet.

Lets say your budget for office supplies is $100 for this month. You just ordered $100 worth of office supplies from a supplier and hence consumed your entire budget. The supplier has not billed you yet. However you have placed an order and hence you are committed to pay. Available funds at this point are still $100. Another person can place another order for $100 worth of supplies and hence actuals would exceed the budget by 100%.

In order to prevent this from happening an encumbrance entry should be recorded at the time the order is placed. The entry would bring the available funds down to zero. Once the supplier bills you, the actual expense is recorded and encumbrance entry is reversed. Available funds would still remain zero. All you are doing is reducing encumbrance and increasing actual in the following equation.

- Available Funds = Actual - Budgets - Encumbrances

If you are using Purchasing and Payables modules then encumbrance entries are automatically generated when purchase orders are created and are automatically reversed once invoices are entered in the system.

Question 99: What are income statement accounts?

Expenses and revenue accounts are called income statement accounts because they appear in income statement reports.

Question 100: What is an income statement report?

An income statement report displays the performance of a company in a particular period. It lists all expense and revenue accounts along with their PTD balances. PTD or period to date balance is a net activity in an account in a particular period.

The report also shows the net income at the end.

- Net Income = Revenue - Expenses

Income statement report is also known as profit and less (P&L) report.

Question 101: What are balance sheet accounts?

Assets, liabilities and owner's equity accounts are called balance sheet accounts because they appear in balance sheet reports.

Question 102: What is a balance sheet report?

A balance sheet report shows health of a company as of a particular period.

Balance sheet report lists all asset, liability, and owner's equity accounts along with their YTD balances. YTD or year-to-date balance is a net activity in an account from the begin of time till the end of a particular period.

The accounting equation, ASSETS - LIABILITIES = OWNER'S EQUITY must remain balanced all the time. Balance sheet report is a good check for that.

Question 103: What would it mean if the accounting equation is not balanced in your balance sheet?

The accounting equation should remain balanced if debits equal to credits for all posted journals. Oracle posting program does not post any journal that violates this rule. If accounting equation is not balanced then the first thing you need to do is check your balance sheet report to see if it is capturing all balance sheet accounts. If report looks fine, then most likely there is a data corruption in your database. Oracle support must be contacted.

Question 104: What are different types of reports that you could run in General Ledger?

Mainly there are two types of reports:

- Standard reports.
- FSG reports, also known an Financial Statement Generator reports or financial reports.

Question 105: What are standard reports?

Standards reports or requests come seeded with Oracle. You can add your own reports as well, however programming skills are required in order to do that. Most of the standard reports are created in Oracle Reports

Designer Tool.

Question 106: What are FSG reports?

FSG stands for Financial Statement Generator. FSG is a tool in Oracle that lets you create reports without writing a single programming code. End users could use this tool to create their own reports. Income statement report, balance sheet report, and cash flow statement are created using FSG tool.

Question 107: What is a cash flow statement?

Cash flow statement displays cash position of a company by listing all cash inflows and outflows during a period along with beginning and ending balances.

Question 108: Give few examples of commonly run standard reports in General Ledger.

Few commonly run standard reports in General Ledger are:

- General Ledger Report: Lists beginning and ending account balances, and all journal entry lines affecting each account balance.
- Account Analysis Report: Lists accumulated balances of a range of accounts and all journal entry lines that affect that range.
- Trial Balance Report: Lists account balances and net activity.
- Journal Report: Lists journal information for posted and unposted journals.

Question 109: Give few examples of commonly run FSG reports that you create in Oracle.

Following two reports must be created in FSG tool:

- Income Statement Report
- Balance Sheet Report

Optionally you could also create Cash Flow Statement.

Question 110: Describe mandatory components of an FSG report.

An FSG report consists of the following mandatory components:

- Row Set: You specify accounts to be displayed. Accounts appear vertically in a report on left side.
- Column Set: You specify the periods and balance types to be displayed. Column titles appear horizontally at top of a report.

At an intersection of a row and a column, Oracle displays an appropriate amount.

In both row set and column set, you can specify formulas as well. For example, you may add a third column in the report that would simply display the sum of first two columns.

Question 111: Describe optional components of an FSG reports.

You can add following optional components to an FSG report.

- Content Set: By attaching a content set to a report you can generate multiple similar reports. For example a report built for one department could be run for all other departments using a content set without having you recreate this report for each department.
- Row Order: Primarily row order is used to control the sorting of data. It can also be used to suppress column headers and value descriptions, and to re-arrange segments.
- Display Set: By attaching a display set to a report you can hide sensitive information from users. Display set hides specified rows, columns, or intersections.

Question 112: What is an FSG report set?

An FSG report set is a group of FSG reports.

If you often run multiple FSG reports then you might want want to create a set and place the frequently run reports within the set. That way all you need to do is run the set and all the reports within the set would be launched simultaneously with one submission.

Question 113: What are three main processes pertaining to foreign currencies in General Ledger module?

Following three key terms are wildly used pertaining to foreign currencies:

- Conversion
- Translation
- Revaluation

Question 114: Explain the process of currency conversion.

Oracle maintains account balances in functional currency. If you enter a foreign currency journal then the amounts must be converted into functional currency at the time of journal entry. That is why you have to provide an exchange rate. Conversion of foreign currency amounts into functional currency at the time of journal entry is called "currency conversion". Conversion is a mandatory action that automatically takes place when you enter a foreign currency journal.

For example, lets say your functional currency is CAD. Mainly you enter journals in CAD. No conversion takes place. One day you did a performed a business transaction with a company in United States and you had to enter a journal in USD. You provided current exchange rate to Oracle at the time of journal entry. Oracle performed the conversion of your journal line amounts from USD to CAD.

Oracle General Ledger R12 Interview Questions by Hasan Mir

Question 115: Explain the process of currency translation.

Financial reports are run against account balances. Account balances are maintained in functional currency. If you wish to run reports in a currency other than functional currency then first you must translate functional currency balances into target foreign currency. Original functional currency balances remain in the system. Translation creates new set of balances in the foreign currency. After the translation, financial reports could be run in a functional currency as well as in the foreign currency. Translation is an optional process that is only run by users if there is a requirement to produce financial reports in a foreign currency.

For example lets say your functional currency is CAD. You primary requirement is to produce reports in CAD. No translation is needed till this point. Lets say a company in the United States is considering to buy your company and you are asked to submit your financial reports in USD. First you will translate your balances into USD. Then you will run your reports in USD and submit them to your potential buyer.

Question 116: Explain the process of currency revaluation.

The purpose of revaluation is to bring the outstanding obligations closer to reality. Lets say if you owe some one $100 USD which amounts to $120 CAD in your functional currency at that moment. The obligation is not settled yet and it is time to run your financial reports. Lets say due to fluctuation in exchange rate your $100 USD loan is now equal to $140 CAD at the time you are running your period end reports. Your reports must show $20 exchange rate loss. The revaluation process would create the exchange rate loss entry and reports would represent the true picture. Same is true if someone owes you in foreign currency amounts.

Usually revaluation is run for accounts payables account (what you owe to others) and accounts receivables account (what others owe you). The final exchange rate gain and loss entries are generated when the obligation is settled. Revaluation entries must be reversed before the obligation is settled. Usually the entries are reversed at the first day of the next period.

Using the same example lets say you finally paid the lender $100 USD which amounts to $160 CAD at that time. $40 loss would be automatically generated by Payables module. That is why revaluation journals generated by General Ledger must be reversed to avoid double counting.

Oracle General Ledger R12 Interview Questions by Hasan Mir

Question 117: What are different exchange rates that are used in conversion, translation, and revaluation?

The conversion process uses spot rate. Current day's rate is also known as spot rate. When you enter a foreign currency journal, you can enter that day's exchange rate manually. If your company is centrally managing the exchanging rates then you can make Oracle fetch that day's rate for you automatically from this predefined exchange rate database.

The Translation process uses three types of exchange rates as required by accounting practices. Balance sheet balances are translated using period end rates. Income statement balances are translated using period average rates. Owner's equity balances are translated using historical exchange rates.

The Revaluation process uses period end rate.

Question 118: Where do you enter daily rates, period end rates, period average rates, and historical rates?

In R12 all exchange rates are entered in Daily Rates screen, except for the historical rate.

You can group different types of rates into "rate types". For example period average rates are entered in a different rate type than daily exchange rates. In 11i there was a separate window to manage period average rates.

Oracle General Ledger R12 Interview Questions by Hasan Mir

Period end rates are simply daily exchange rates as of period ends.

There is a separate screen for managing historical rates called Historical Rates screen. You can either enter the historical rates for selected accounts or you can enter actual historical amounts instead as well.

Question 119: What are rate types?

If your company uses more than one version of daily rates, then you can create multiple rate types and enter different rates in each rate type for the same currency pair. This way you would have multiple databases of exchange rates. Each group can refer to the rate type of their choice while entering foreign currency journals or when performing translations and revaluations.

Question 120: How would you perform consolidated reporting of two companies?

Consolidated reporting could be done in two ways:

- FSG reports could be created to display consolidated data of two companies. This is only possible if both companies are sharing the same ledger. If the two companies are residing in their own ledger then displaying consolidated amounts in FSG reports is still possible if the two companies are sharing the same data access set.
- The other way is to copy the data, either in summary or detailed mode, from subsidiary ledger to parent ledger and then run the reports from

parent ledger. Oracle provides a consolidation workbench to manage copying of data from one ledger to the other. The process is called consolidation data transfer.

Question 121: What are the steps involved in performing a consolidation data transfer from one ledger to the other?

Following high level steps are required in order to perform a consolidation data transfer:

- You create a chart of account mapping between the subsidiary and parent chart of account structures.
- Once the mapping is ready, consolidation definition is created where you specify the names of parent and subsidiary ledgers and other transfer options like summary or detailed transfer etc.
- You run the data transfer.
- You review generated journals in parent ledger.
- You post journals in parent ledger.

Question 122: Why is mapping required for consolidation data transfer?

Chart of account structure could be different in parent ledger and subsidiary ledger. Not only that, segment values could be different as well.

For example lets say cash account in subsidiary ledger is 01-1000 and the cash account in parent ledger is 10-1100-00. The structure of the subsidiary is COMPANY-ACCOUNT while the structure of the parent is COMPANY-ACCOUNT-REGION. Due to the difference in structure and in values a mapping must be provided. Based on the mapping, Oracle determines to which target account in parent should the balance be transferred from the source account in subsidiary.

Question 123: Explain elimination entries using an example?

Lets say one subsidiary company sells some service to a sister company. This transaction is recorded as a revenue for one and an expense for the other. At month end both subsidiary companies send over accounting data to their parent company. The parent company is not interested in displaying in its reports the revenue and expense activity associated with that particular transaction that took place between its children companies. Hence the parent company would pass an entry to eliminate these transactions from its ledger. This entry is called an elimination entry.

Elimination entries are passed to nullify the effect of transactions on the parent income statement that took place among children companies.

Question 124: Explain average balancing?

Financial institutions have a requirement to submit average balance sheet reports in addition to standard balance sheet. Average balance sheet reports display average balances as opposed to period end balances.

An average balance is computed as the sum of the daily closing balances for the period divided by the number of days in that period.

Once you enable average balancing, Oracle automatically maintains average balances.

Question 125: What does freezing a source means in Oracle General Ledger?

When you freeze a source then that means journals coming into General Ledger from that source cannot be reverses or deleted. As a result that external module remain in sync with General Ledger.

Question 126: What features are available in Account Inquiry screen for end-users?

Account inquiry window lets you query any type of account balances, and lets you perform variance analysis between actual balances and budget balances or between two different budget versions. It also lets you drill down from balances into journal details.

Question 127: What is the significance of sequences in Oracle General Ledger module?

Sequences are simply automatic numbering of journals to comply with legal requirements in some countries e.g. Italy.

It allows fiscal authorities to verify the completeness of a company's accounting records.

Question 128: Explain the types of sequences available in release R12.

There are two types of sequences available:

- Accounting Sequence: Unique sequence number is assigned to a journal when the journal is posted.
- Reporting Sequence: Unique sequence number is assigned to a journal when the period is closed.

Both sequences are mutually exclusive. You can use both together if you wish.

Question 129: What is the significance of journal approval feature?

Journal approval feature lets you ensure that journals are first approved by the appropriate manager before they are posted. This feature uses Oracle Workflow module to send notifications.

Question 130: What are the setup steps involved in enabling journal approvals?

Following are the high level steps that are needed in order to enable journal approvals:

- Enable journal approvals at your ledger.
- Enable journal approvals for required sources.
- Create an approval hierarchy and define authorization limits.

Question 131: What is a suspense account?

You cannot post a journal unless all debits equal all credits within that journal. If you enable the suspense account feature, then it will allow you to post journals even if debits and credits amount are not equal. The difference between debits and credits would be placed in the suspense account and hence the journal would become balanced.

You can define one suspense account at the ledger level. You can also specify different suspense accounts for each combination of journal source and category. If suspense account feature is enabled then accountants must take measures to review the balance in suspense account periodically and take actions accordingly.

Question 132: What is an Account Hierarchy Manager?

Account Hierarchy Manager is a graphical tool that lets you create, maintain, and review values in your chart of account segments.

Question 133: What are summary accounts?

A summary account is an account whose balance is the sum of balances from multiple detail accounts. Mainly summary accounts are used to perform online inquiries. Summary accounts could also be used in FSG reports, mass allocation formulas, and recurring journal formulas, to speed up the processing. Summary accounts cannot be used directly in journal entries.

Question 134: How do you create summary accounts?

You create a summary account template in Oracle. Based on this template Oracle creates summary accounts. You do not create summary accounts directly.

Question 135: Lets say you are asked to create summary accounts so that one can query consolidated balances in all assets for each individual company. How would you go about that task assuming a two segment chart of account structure: COMPANY-ACCOUNT?

Steps to create summary accounts are as follows:

- Create a parent value, say AA, representing all assets. This value is created in a value set associated with the account segment.
- Assign all the detail asset accounts to the parent value AA. This can be done by specifying a range, say from 1000 to 1999.
- Create a rollup group. We can call this rollup group AA as well.
- Assign the parent value representing all assets, AA, to the rollup AA.
- Create a summary account template using the value: D-AA. D meaning we need details at company segment and AA meaning we need summary by total assets at account segment.
- This template would create as many summary accounts as there are companies in the company segment. Lets say there are two companies 01 and 02 then Oracle would create two summary

accounts: 01-AA and 02-AA.
- Now users could perform inquiries on accounts 01-AA and 02-AA just the way they would perform inquires on any other account. Balance in 01-AA would be equal to the total balance of all company 01 asset accounts. Similarly balance in 02-AA would equal to the total balance of all company 02 asset accounts.

Question 136:   What formula values you can enter in a summary account template.

You can use following values in a summary account template:

- D: Each child value would be retained.
- T: All child values group be consolidated into a value T.
- Rollup Groups: All child values would be consolidated by parent values within this rollup group.

Rollup group must be created before creating a summary template.

As many summary accounts would be created out of this template as the number of child values in D segment.

Question 137:   What is a parent value?

A parent value is a value that has one or more children values associated with it. Parent value is created in the same value set as the children values.

Parent values cannot be used in a journal entry.

Question 138: What is a rollup group?

A rollup group is simply a collection of related parent values. A rollup group allows you to group related parent values for creating summary templates.

Question 139: Can you use a parent value directly in summary account template instead of using a rollup group?

Only rollup groups could be used in summary account templates. You must create a rollup group, even though it might contain only one parent value.

Question 140: Can a child value belong to more than one parent value?

Yes a child value can be assigned to more than one parent value. For example, you can create a parent value representing all liquid assets and another parent value representing all assets. Both the parents would include child values for cash account, for example.

Alphabetical Index

4 Cs	20
4 Cs vs 3 Cs	22
Account Balances	45
Account Combinations	39
Account Hierarchy Manager	77
Account Inquiry Screen	75
Accounting Convention	22
Accounting Convention - Accrual vs Cash	22
Accounting Equation Not Balanced	64
Accounting Flexfield	26
Adjustment Period	34
Available Funds	61
Average Balancing	74
Balance Sheet Accounts	63
Balance Sheet Report	63
Balancing Segment	31
Budget Formula	56
Budget Formula vs Recurring Journals	56
Budget Groups	60
Budget Organization	57
Budget Organization Validation	58

Oracle General Ledger R12 Interview Questions by Hasan Mir

Budgets..54

Budgets Setup...57

Calendar - Future Years..32

Calendar - Past Years..33

Calendar Setup...31

Calendar Validation..33

Cash Flow Statement..65

Chart of Account Structure Maximum Number of Segments...............24

Chart of Account Structure Minimum Number of Segments...............24

Chart of Account Structure Multiple Segments....................23

Chart of Account Structure Planning....................................26

Chart of Account Structure Redundant Segments................25

Chart of Account Structure Segments Examples..................25

Chart of Account Structure Setup...28

Consolidated Reporting..72

Consolidation Mapping..73

Consolidation Process..73

Creation Budget Journal Options..59

Cross Validation Rule...40

Cross Validation Rule and GL Accounts Screen..................41

Cross Validation Rules Example...42

Currency Conversion..68

Currency Conversion, Translation, Revaluation...................68

Oracle General Ledger R12 Interview Questions by Hasan Mir

Currency Revaluation..69

Currency Translation..69

Data Access Set..36

Data Access Set Restrictions..37

Data Flow into General Ledger..17, 46

Debits and Credits..21

Dynamic Insertion...40

Dynamic Insertion and Cross Validation Rules Setup...............41

Elimination Entries...74

Encumbrance..61

Entering Budget Amounts Options..59

Entering Budgets Options..58

ERP...16

Exchange Rate Options..71

Exchange Rate Types...71

Flexfields..26

Flexfields Types - Key and Descriptive....................................26

Foreign Currency Journal - Entering...35

Foreign Currency Journal - Providing Exchange Rates............35

FSG Report Mandatory Components...66

FSG Report Optional Components..67

FSG Report Set..67

FSG Reports...65

83

Oracle General Ledger R12 Interview Questions by Hasan Mir

FSG Reports Examples..66

Functional Currency..35

Functional Currency Setup...34

Fund Check Level..60

General Ledger Cycle..47

General Ledger Functionality...16

General Ledger Module...16

General Ledger Setup...18

GL Acccounts Screen Significance..39

GL Interface...46

Income Statement Accounts..62

Income Statement Report...63

Journal Approval..76

Journal Approval Setup...76

Journal Batches Creation..36

Journal Creation...47

Journal Deletion...43

Journal Hierarchy - Batches, Journals, Lines..................................36

Journal Lines Debits and Credits..36

Journal Posting..43

Journal Posting Options..45

Journal Reversal..43

Journal Reversal Methods...44

Oracle General Ledger R12 Interview Questions by Hasan Mir

Journal Reversal Options...44

Journal Reversal vs Deletion..43

Journal Sequence Types...76

Journal Sequences..75

Journal Source Freeze..75

Journal Types...54

Journal Validation..54

Key vs Descriptive Flexfields..27

Ledger...18

Ledger - Multiple Companies..29

Ledger Components...19

Ledger Setup...20

Legal Entity..19

Legal Entity and Ledger...19

Mass Allocation..52

Mass Allocation vs MassBudget..55

MassBudget..55

Oracle E-Business Suite...16

Oracle Financials..16

Parent and Child Values...80

Parent Value...79

Period Statuses...48

PTD vs YTD..45

Oracle General Ledger R12 Interview Questions by Hasan Mir

Rate Types..72

Recurring Journal...53

Release R12 New Features..48

Retained Earnings Account...20

Rollup Group...80

Secondary Ledger vs Reporting Ledger...52

Security Rules...38

Security Rules Creation...38

Security Rules vs Data Access Set..37p.

Segment Qualifier..31

Standard Reports...64

Standard Reports Examples..65

STAT Journal Creation Options..53

Summary Account Template and Rollup Groups................................80

Summary Accounts..77

Summary Accounts Creation..78

Summary Accounts Example..78

Summary Accounts Template Options..79

Suspense Account...77

Types of Accounts...21

Types of Reports...64

Value Set...29

Value Set and Segments..29

Value Set Significance..29

Made in the USA
Lexington, KY
20 August 2011